POPE FRANCIS

YOUR FIRST
COMMUNION

 Meeting Jesus, Your True Joy

MAGNIFICAT · Ignatius

Children are the ones
Jesus loves most!
Jesus loves us very much.
All of us! He is close to us
and walks with us through life —
when we are sad
and when we have problems.
Jesus is always close to us!

Pope Francis

CONTENTS

God Is Our Creator
Who Loves Us Totally

I ask you children: "Who knows who God is?" Raise your hand.
Tell me? There! Creator of the earth. And how many Gods are there?
One? But I have been told that there are three: the Father,
the Son and the Holy Spirit! How can this be explained? Is there
one or are there three? One? One? And how is it possible
to explain that one is the Father, another the Son and the other
the Holy Spirit? They are three in one, three Persons in one.

And what does the Father do? The Father is the beginning,
the Father who created all things, who created us. What does the
Son do? What does Jesus do? Does he love us? And then? He brings
the word of God! Jesus comes to teach us the word of God.
This is excellent! And what then? What did Jesus do on earth?
He saved us! And Jesus came to give his life for us.
The Father creates the world; Jesus saves us.

And what does the Holy Spirit do? He loves us! He gives you love!
The Father creates all, he creates the world; Jesus saves us; and
the Holy Spirit? He loves us! And this is Christian life: talking
to the Father, talking to the Son and talking to the Holy Spirit.

MEETING JESUS IN HOLY COMMUNION

Jesus Gives Us Strength in the Eucharist — Holy Communion

Jesus has saved us, but he also walks beside us in life. He walks with us, he helps us, he leads us and he teaches us to journey on.

And Jesus also gives us the strength to work. And also in our school tasks! He supports us, he helps us, he leads us. How does Jesus give us strength? You know this, you know that in Communion he gives us strength. It seems to be bread. It is not really bread. What is it? It is the Body of Jesus. Jesus comes into our hearts.

Meeting Jesus—
The Most Important Thing in Life

The most important thing that can happen to a person is to meet Jesus. Jesus loves us, he saved us, he has given his life for us.

We could ask ourselves this question: But when do I meet Jesus? Only at the end? No, no! We meet him every day. How? In prayer, when you pray, you meet Jesus. When you receive Communion, you meet Jesus. Our whole life is meetings with Jesus: in prayer, when we go to Mass, and when we do good works—when we visit the sick, when we help the poor, when we think of others, when we are not selfish, when we are loving—in these things we always meet Jesus. And the journey of life is precisely this: journeying in order to meet Jesus.

Sunday — The Most Important Day for Christians

Dear friends, we don't ever thank the Lord enough for the gift he has given us in the Eucharist! It is a very great gift, and that is why it is so important to go to Mass on Sunday. Go to Mass not just to pray, but to receive Communion, the bread that is the Body of Jesus Christ, who saves us, forgives us, unites us to the Father. It is a beautiful thing to do! And we go to Mass every Sunday because that is the day of the resurrection of the Lord. That is why Sunday is so important to us.

Our Joy Comes from Communion with Jesus

Here is the first word that I wish to say to you: joy! Do not be sad. Never give way to discouragement! Ours is not a joy born of having many things, but of meeting a Person: Jesus, in our midst. It is born of knowing that with him we are never alone, even at difficult moments, even when we have problems that seem too big for us, and there are so many of them! In these moments the enemy, the devil, comes, often disguised as an angel, and slyly speaks to us. Do not listen to him! Let us follow Jesus! We go with Jesus, but above all we know that he goes with us and carries us on his shoulders. This is our joy; this is the hope that we must bring to this world.

THE POWER OF
THE SACRAMENTS
AND THE LIGHT
OF CHRIST

The Strength of Baptism and the Eucharist Makes Us Better People

Baptism makes us children of God. The Eucharist unites us to Christ. Both sacraments must be expressed in our attitudes, behavior, gestures and decisions. If I let myself be touched by the grace of the Risen Christ, if I let him change in me that aspect of mine which is not good or which can hurt me and others, I allow the victory of Christ to have power in my life. This is the power of God's grace! Without his grace we can do nothing. And with the grace of Baptism and of Eucharistic Communion I can become an instrument of God's mercy.

Baptism—
A New Life in Christ

A baptized child and an unbaptized child are not the same. A person who is baptized and a person who is not baptized are not the same. We, by Baptism, are immersed in that infinite source of life, which is the death of Jesus, the greatest act of love in all of history. Thanks to this love we can live a new life, no longer at the mercy of evil, of sin and of death, but in communion with God and with our brothers and sisters.

Living Our Baptism Every Day

We are called to live out our Baptism every day. At our Baptism we have become new creatures and have been clothed in Christ. That is why we manage to follow Jesus and his Church despite our weaknesses and our sins. It is by the power of Baptism, in fact, that, freed of original sin, we are children of God the Father; that we are bearers of a new hope, for Baptism gives us this new hope: the hope of going on the path of salvation our whole life long. And this hope nothing and no one can extinguish, for it is a hope that does not disappoint. Remember, hope in the Lord never disappoints. Thanks to Baptism, we are capable of forgiving and of loving even those who offend us and do evil to us. By our Baptism, we recognize in the least and in the poor the face of the Lord, who visits us and makes himself close. Baptism helps us to recognize in the face of the needy, the suffering, and also of our neighbor, the face of Jesus. All this is possible thanks to the power of Baptism!

Jesus — The Way of Salvation and the Light of Life

Jesus tells us that there is a door which opens to God's family, to the warmth of God's house. This door is Jesus himself. He is the door. He is the way to salvation. He leads us to the Father, and the door that is Jesus is never closed. Jesus is waiting for you to embrace you, to pardon you. Do not be afraid: he is waiting for you. Jesus is a light that never goes out. It is not a firework, not a flash of light! No, it is a peaceful light that lasts for ever and gives us peace. It is this light that greets us when we enter through Jesus' door.

HOLY CONFESSION—MEETING CHRIST WHO LOVES US DEARLY

God Is Patient as He Awaits Us

Look how God works: he is not impatient like us, who often want everything all at once. God is patient with us because he loves us, and those who love are able to understand, to hope, to inspire confidence; they do not give up, they are able to forgive. Let us remember this in our lives as Christians: God always waits for us, even when we have left him behind! He is never far from us, and if we return to him, he is ready to embrace us.

God is always waiting for us; he never grows tired. Jesus shows us this merciful patience of God so that we can regain confidence, hope and love! This is important: the courage to trust in Jesus' mercy.

In my own life, I have so often seen God's merciful look, his patience; I have also seen so many people find the courage to enter the wounds of Jesus by saying to him: "Lord, I am here, accept my poverty, hide my sin in your wounds, wash it away with your blood." And I have always seen that God did just this—he accepted them, consoled them, cleansed them and loved them. Let us be enveloped by the mercy of God. Let us trust in his patience, which always gives us more time. Let us find the courage to return to his house, to dwell in his loving wounds, allowing ourselves be loved by him and to encounter his mercy in the sacraments. We will feel his wonderful tenderness, we will feel his embrace, and we too will become more capable of mercy, patience, forgiveness and love.

God Forgives Us Our Sins and Is Tender like a Good Father

We all have some darkness in our lives. When we are too full of ourselves, when we are convinced that we do not need to be saved, then we walk in darkness. When one keeps on following the paths leading into the darkness, it is not easy to go back. If we claim we are without sin, we deceive ourselves. Look at your sins, our sins: we are sinners, all of us! This is the starting point. However, if we confess our sins, God is so faithful that he forgives them and washes them away. He himself came to save us, so when he forgives us, he is faithful to himself! As a father is tender to his children so is the Lord to those who fear him, to those who go to him. The tenderness of the Lord is so great! With it I am serene, I go in peace, in the peace that only he gives. It is what occurs in the Sacrament of Reconciliation.

Jesus Awaits Us to Forgive Us

We think that going to confession is the same as going to
the dry cleaner's.

But Jesus in the confessional is not a dry cleaner's.
A confession is an appointment with Jesus,
who embraces us the way we are. We can say to him:
"Lord, listen, I am this way." We are ashamed to tell
the truth: I did this, I thought about this. However,
shame is a true virtue, both Christian and human,
a virtue of humble people.

The Helper (the Holy Spirit) is by our side and supports us in front of the Father. Now, how should we go to meet him? Like this, recognizing humbly that we are sinners, with confidence and with cheerfulness, without any pretending. We must never put on a mask in front of God! We must be truthful! Do you feel ashamed? Shame is a blessing! It is a virtue. This is the virtue we are asked for by Jesus: humility and meekness.

Humility and meekness—they are like the frames of a Christian life. A Christian always goes with humility and meekness. Jesus awaits us in order to forgive us. We could ask: "Is going to confession like going to a punishment?" No! It is going to praise God because I, a sinner, have been saved by him. Is he awaiting me to give me a beating? No. He awaits tenderly to forgive me. What if I do the same sin tomorrow? Go to confession again, go over and over again. He will always be waiting for us. The Lord is so full of tenderness, humility, and meekness—this allows us to breathe. May the Lord grant us the grace and the courage to go in front of him always with the truth, because the truth is the light, and not with the darkness of half-truths and lies. May the Lord grant us this grace.

THE CHURCH IS LIKE A MOTHER

The Church Tenderly Teaches Us How to Walk through Life

What does a mother do?

First of all, she teaches how to walk through life, she teaches the right path to take through life, she knows how to guide her children, she always tries to point out to them the right path for growing up and becoming adults. And she does so with tenderness, affection and love, even when she is trying to straighten out our path because we are going a little astray in life or taking roads that lead to danger. A mother knows what's important for a child to enable him to walk the right way through life. Moreover she did not learn it from books but from her own heart. The university of mothers is their hearts. They learn there how to bring up their children.

The Church does the same thing: she gives our life direction, she instructs us so that we can follow the right path. A mother never teaches what is evil; she only wants the good of her children and so does the Church.

She Understands,
Gives Encouragement and
Offers God's Forgiveness

A mother has patience for her children, always and in every situation. With the force of her love, a mother can follow her children on their way with discretion and tenderness. Even when they go astray, she always finds a way to understand them, to be close, to help.

This is how the Church is. She is a merciful mother who understands, who always seeks to help and to encourage even those of her children who have acted badly or who are making mistakes. She never closes the door to home. She does not judge but offers God's forgiveness. She offers his love, which invites even those of her children who are lost to continue on their way. The Church is not afraid to enter their darkness to give them hope. Because the Church is mother!

She Prays for Us and Gives Us to the Lord

A last thought: for her children a mother is also able to ask and to knock at every door, without calculation; she does so out of love. And I think of how mothers can also and especially knock at the door of God's heart! Mothers say so many prayers for their children, especially for the weaker ones, for those in the greatest need or who have gone down dangerous or mistaken paths in life.

The Church does this too: with prayers she puts in the Lord's hands all the situations of her children. Let us trust in the power of the prayer of Mother Church, who knows the Lord cares for us. He always knows how to amaze us when we least expect it, as Mother Church knows!

Let us see the Church as a good mother who points out to us the way through life, who is always patient, merciful, understanding and who knows how to put us in God's hands.

MESSAGES FOR LIFE

Do Not Be Afraid to Dream of Great Things!

I ask you who are just setting out on your journey through life: Have you thought about the talents God has given you? Have you thought of how you can put them at the service of others? Do not bury your talents! Set your stakes on great ideals, the ideals that enlarge the heart, the ideals of service that make your talents fruitful. Life is not given to us to be jealously guarded for ourselves, but is given to us so that we may give it in turn. Dear young people, have a deep spirit! Do not be afraid to dream of great things!

Be Generous!

We must be generous, with a big heart, without fear; always betting on the great ideals. Greatness also exists in doing little things, daily things, with a big heart, a great heart. It is important to find this generosity with Jesus. Jesus is the One who opens windows for us on the horizon. Greatness comes from walking with Jesus, with a heart attentive to what he tells us.

Do Not Let Yourselves Be Robbed of Hope!

Please, do not let yourselves be robbed of hope! And who robs you of hope? The spirit of the world, wealth, the spirit of vanity, arrogance, pride. All these things steal hope from you. Where do I find hope? In the poor Jesus, Jesus who made himself poor for us. But do not let yourselves be robbed of hope by the spirit of self-satisfaction, which in the end leads you to become nothing. The young must stake themselves on high ideals!

Choose True Happiness— Choose Jesus!

If you are really open to the deepest desires of your hearts, you will realize that you possess an unquenchable thirst for happiness, and this will allow you to reject the "low-cost" offers all around you. When we look only for success, pleasure and possessions, we are never satisfied, but always looking for more. It is a tragic thing to see a young person who "has everything", but is weary and weak. Young people who choose Christ are strong: they are fed by his word and they do not need to "stuff themselves" with other things! Have the courage to swim against the tide. Have the courage to be truly happy!

Meeting Jesus, Your true Joy

Write on this page your very own prayer to Jesus.

Memories of My First Communion

My dearest Mary,

Jesus loves you
and He shows it by
giving you life to have
the Gift of Eternal Life
one day soon with Him
in our Eternal Home
along with Mother Mary
and Saint Joseph awaiting us!

In the Love of Jesus through Mary,
Schwartz